Cerebral Palsy

by Judith Peacock

Consultant:
Murray Goldstein, DO, MPH
Medical and Research Director
United Cerebral Palsy Research and Educational Foundation

Perspectives on Disease and Illness

LifeMatters
an imprint of Capstone Press
Mankato, Minnesota

mw

LifeMatters books are published by Capstone Press
818 North Willow Street • Mankato, Minnesota 56001
http://www.capstone-press.com

Printed in the United States of America

Library of Congress Cataloging-in-Publication Data
Peacock, Judith, 1942–
      Cerebral palsy / by Judith Peacock.
          p.   cm. — (Perspectives on disease and illness)
      Includes bibliographical references and index.
      Summary: Discusses the causes, diagnosis, symptoms, and treatment of cerebral palsy, as well as current research and possible ways of preventing this disorder.
      ISBN 0-7368-0280-0 (book). — ISBN 0-7368-0294-0 (series)
      1. Cerebral palsy Juvenile literature. [1. Cerebral palsy.]
      I. Title. II. Series.
      RC388.P43 2000
      616.8′36—DC21   99-31228
                                             CIP

Staff Credits
Kristin Thoennes, Rebecca Aldridge, editors; Adam Lazar, designer; Kimberly Danger, photo researcher

Photo Credits
Cover: Transparencies Inc./©Tom & Dee Ann McCarthy, bottom; PNI/©Digital Vision, left, right; PNI/©Rubberball, middle
©James L. Shaffer, 50
Unicorn Stock Photos/©14; ©B.W. Hoffmann, 22; ©Jean Higgins, 25; ©Aneal F. Vohra, 39; ©Jeff Greenberg, 55
Uniphoto Picture Agency/8, 21, 34, 48, 57; ©Jackson Smith, 58; ©Rick Brady, 47; ©Bob Daemmrich, 42
Visuals Unlimited/11; ©L. Bassett, 6; ©Jeff Greenberg, 17, 31, 33, 40

A 0 9 8 7 6 5 4 3 2

Table of Contents

Chapter Overview

Cerebral palsy is a motor, or movement, disorder. People with cerebral palsy have difficulty with muscle control and coordination. The motor control areas of their brain are permanently damaged.

Cerebral palsy affects people differently. It can cause mild, moderate, or severe motor problems.

People with cerebral palsy may have additional problems. These problems may include seizures, mental retardation, and vision or hearing loss.

Cerebral palsy affects the developing brain. Cerebral palsy usually occurs before, during, or shortly after birth. It also may occur in early childhood.

There are many possible causes of cerebral palsy. No single cause or event is responsible for all occurrences of this condition.

Premature and low birth-weight babies and babies born during multiple births have a higher risk of having cerebral palsy than other babies.

Chapter 1

What Is Cerebral Palsy?

Rodney has cerebral palsy, which makes it hard for him to walk. He uses a powered wheelchair to go to school and other places. Rodney likes to race his wheelchair around the neighborhood. His friends call him "Hot Rod."

Rodney, Age 13

A Motor Disorder

Cerebral palsy is a name for a variety of motor disorders. The word *motor* means "movement." People with cerebral palsy have poor muscle control and coordination. Their arms or legs may have spastic, or tight and stiff, muscles. Their body may move in abnormal ways. They also may have difficulty speaking or swallowing. They may have poor balance as well.

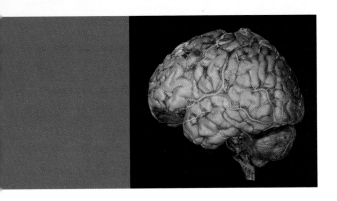

The word *cerebral* refers to the brain. The word *palsy* refers to weakness of the muscles. The brain's motor centers normally control the muscles. The brain sends messages to the spinal cord. The spinal cord relays the messages to the nerves that lead to the muscles. People with cerebral palsy have motor problems because of damage to the brain's motor centers.

Cerebral palsy is a complicated disorder. It affects people differently. Just a small number of people with cerebral palsy are severely affected. More people are affected only mildly or moderately. The severity depends on how much of the brain is damaged. It also depends on the location of the damage.

Nell and Mandy, Ages 17 and 14

Nell is a high school senior with mild cerebral palsy. She walks with a slight limp. Nell is a straight-A student. Her favorite subjects are history and math. Nell is on her school's swim team. Her teammates elected her co-captain. Nell plans to go to college in the fall. She wants to be a psychologist.

Mandy has severe cerebral palsy. She cannot hold her head up, sit up, or use her hands. She cannot walk, talk, or read. Mandy must be fed through a tube in her stomach. She drools and wears diapers. Mandy requires constant care from her family and from home health aides.

Cerebral Palsy

Fact: Cerebral palsy and mental retardation are
different disabilities. The same person may or
may not have both. Most people with cerebral
palsy have normal intelligence.

What Cerebral Palsy Is Not

The following list describes some characteristics that do not apply
to cerebral palsy.

Cerebral palsy is not a disease. People with cerebral palsy
are as healthy as anybody else. It is more accurate to refer to
cerebral palsy as a condition.

Cerebral palsy does not get worse, and it does not get better.
The brain damage happens once and leaves its mark. The
disabilities resulting from cerebral palsy can get better or
worse over time.

Cerebral palsy is not curable. Once the brain has been
damaged, it cannot repair itself. Cerebral palsy is a chronic,
or lifelong, condition.

Cerebral palsy is not contagious. It cannot be spread from
person to person like a cold or the flu. It is not inherited.
People with cerebral palsy need not worry about passing it
on to their children. In rare instances, however, the condition
that caused the cerebral palsy can occur in families.

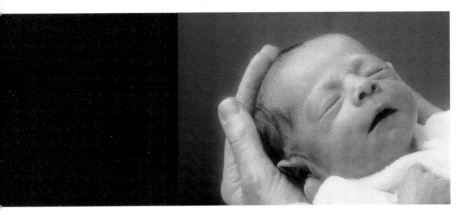

Related Conditions

People with cerebral palsy have muscle weakness and poor muscle control. They often have other problems as well. This is not surprising. When one part of the brain is damaged, it is likely that other parts are damaged, too. People with cerebral palsy may have seizures. Their vision and hearing may be impaired. They may have mental retardation or other learning disabilities. Some people with cerebral palsy have emotional and behavioral problems.

Causes of Cerebral Palsy

Cerebral palsy affects the developing brain. The damage can occur before, during, or shortly after birth. This accounts for about 90 percent of all cases of cerebral palsy. The damage also can occur during early childhood. This accounts for about 10 percent of all cases.

Causes of Cerebral Palsy During Pregnancy

Doctors and scientists often cannot identify the specific reason cerebral palsy occurs during pregnancy. There are many possible causes. These include:

A defect in the structure of the brain

Exposure of the mother to infections such as German measles or herpes

Exposure of the mother to poisonous chemicals

Diseases that the mother has, such as diabetes or anemia

A lack of nourishment in the mother

Physical injury to the mother

Too little oxygen reaching the infant's brain during pregnancy or labor

Injury during delivery

Cerebral palsy used to be called "Little's Disease." This name comes from William Little, a British doctor. During the mid-1800s, Dr. Little identified cerebral palsy as a separate condition. He showed how it was different from other physical and mental disabilities.

Causes of Cerebral Palsy During Infancy

Cerebral palsy in infancy may result from any of the following:

Head injury from a car accident, a fall, or child abuse

Infections of the brain

Exposure to poisonous chemicals (lead, household cleaning materials, medications, alcohol, street drugs)

Severe malnutrition and neglect

Repeated severe seizures

Motor disorders may appear for the first time in older children or in adults. These problems are not cerebral palsy. Instead, brain infection, stroke, or head injury might cause them. Cerebral palsy is a condition of the developing brain. The developmental period for motor abilities generally lasts from age two until age seven or eight.

Premature and Multiple Births

There are many unanswered questions about the causes of cerebral palsy. Doctors and researchers know one thing for sure. Premature babies are at greater risk for cerebral palsy than full-term babies. The risk increases as the birth weight decreases. The heart and lungs of premature babies may not be fully developed. They may have breathing problems. Premature babies with low birth weight can have bleeding into the brain. This internal bleeding may damage the motor areas.

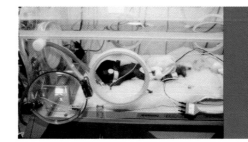

Rick has a moderate form of cerebral palsy.
He was born 10 weeks premature. He

Rick, Age 12

weighed 2 pounds 5 ounces at birth. His birth weight quickly
dropped to 1 pound 15 ounces and he had bleeding inside his
brain. Rick was rushed to a special unit for newborns at a
children's hospital. He spent the first nine weeks of his life in
the hospital. When he was strong enough, his parents brought
him home.

Babies born during multiple births also are at a higher risk for
cerebral palsy than babies born during single births. Multiple
births are those in which more than one child is born at one time.
Twins are an example of a multiple birth.

Points to Consider

What information would you be able to give to
someone who didn't know much about cerebral palsy?

Do you know anyone who has cerebral palsy? Are
there students in your school with cerebral palsy? How
do you know?

How do you react to people with disabilities?

Chapter Overview

Cerebral palsy is classified in two main ways. One way involves how cerebral palsy affects movement. The other way involves which part of the body is affected. The two ways of describing cerebral palsy often are combined.

Spastic, athetoid, and ataxic describe how cerebral palsy affects movement.

Monoplegia, diplegia, triplegia, quadriplegia, and hemiplegia describe which part of the body is affected.

Chapter 2

Types of Cerebral Palsy

There are several different forms of cerebral palsy. They are usually classified, or grouped, in two ways. One way is according to how movement is affected. Another way is according to which part of the body is most affected.

Effect on Movement

The following types of cerebral palsy influence movement:

Spastic Cerebral Palsy

This type, which is most common, involves poor signals from the brain to the spinal cord. Nerves in the spine act on their own. They tell some muscles to contract. The muscles become tight and stiff and then suddenly relax. People with spastic cerebral palsy have a hard time moving their arms or legs.

Athetoid Cerebral Palsy

In this type, the muscles are in constant motion. Arms, legs, head, and other body parts move in an uncontrolled way. The person's body may twist and turn and jerk suddenly. Muscles in the face are affected, too. The person may appear to be making faces.

Ataxic Cerebral Palsy

This type disturbs balance. People with ataxic cerebral palsy may sway back and forth when standing. They may walk with their feet wide apart to avoid falling.

Hypotonic Cerebral Palsy

In this type, the muscles are weak and floppy.

Hypertonic (rigid) Cerebral Palsy

This type is like spastic cerebral palsy. The muscles become extremely tight.

It is not always easy to say which type of cerebral palsy a person has. A person may have more than one type. A person's symptoms may change from time to time. There are widely varying degrees of each type. For example, a person may have mild, moderate, or severe spastic cerebral palsy. Doctors try to identify the main type. This helps them decide how to manage the condition.

Did You
Know?

Cerebral palsy severely affected Irish writer-artist Christy Brown. He could control only one part of his body. That was his left foot. Brown used his foot to paint wonderful pictures. Read his amazing autobiography, *My Left Foot,* or rent the movie version from your local video store.

Cindy's cerebral palsy is mainly the athetoid type. Her arms and legs move in ways she cannot control. She must use a wheelchair to get around. Cindy speaks very slowly and carefully. Sometimes she drools. People who don't know her think she is retarded. People who take the time to listen find out something different. They learn that Cindy is smart and funny.

Cindy, Age 16

Effect on Body Parts

The following terms describe how cerebral palsy affects certain body parts:

Monoplegia—one arm or leg is affected. The prefix *mono-* means "one."

Diplegia—both arms or both legs are affected. The prefix *di-* means "two."

Triplegia—three limbs are affected (for example, both legs and an arm). The prefix *tri-* means "three."

Quadriplegia—both arms and both legs and usually the trunk are affected. The prefix *quad-* means "four."

Hemiplegia—an arm and a leg on the same side of the body are affected. The prefix *hemi-* means "half."

The United States Cerebral Palsy Athletic Association sponsors competitions for athletes with cerebral palsy. It has another way of classifying cerebral palsy. The organization uses an eight-level classification system. An athlete is assigned a level that fits his or her ability to perform. Athletes compete against other athletes at the same level. This makes the competition fair.

Combined Description

The two ways of classifying cerebral palsy often are combined. A person might have spastic diplegia or spastic hemiplegia, for example. There are a number of possible combinations.

Kids With Cerebral Palsy

Shyanna has spastic hemiplegia. Her right arm and right leg are curled, or contracted. She holds her arm close to her body. Her hand bends down at the wrist. She cannot hold anything with that hand. When Shyanna walks, she steps hard on her left foot. Only the toes on her right foot touch the ground.

Trent has spastic diplegia. He tends to stand on his toes. When he walks, his lower legs turn in and cross at the ankles. This is called the scissors gait. Most of the time, Trent can keep up with his friends. When they walk long distances, Trent uses crutches or a wheelchair.

Kareem has spastic quadriplegia. Spasticity affects all parts of his body. Spasticity in the muscles of his face and throat makes it hard to eat and talk. Spasticity in his trunk makes it hard to sit. Kareem must use a special wheelchair.

Points to Consider

What is one advantage of classifying cerebral palsy into different types? What is one disadvantage?

What does it mean if someone calls you a "spaz" or "spastic"? How would you feel if you had cerebral palsy and someone called you those names?

Have you ever met someone who had difficulty speaking? How did you react?

Chapter Overview

Some children with cerebral palsy show symptoms in infancy. Others do not show symptoms until they are older.

Lack of muscle control and poor coordination are the main signs of cerebral palsy. Doctors pay close attention to a child's motor development when diagnosing cerebral palsy.

Diagnosis of cerebral palsy involves several steps. These include a medical history, a physical examination, and various tests.

Diagnosing cerebral palsy can be difficult. There is no test for cerebral palsy. The symptoms are similar to those of other conditions.

The sooner cerebral palsy can be detected the better. Early intervention can reduce the child's developmental disabilities.

Chapter 3

Diagnosing Cerebral Palsy

Early detection of cerebral palsy can lead to early treatment. The child will have a better chance to grow and develop.

Symptoms of Cerebral Palsy

Ron and Carly happily announced the birth of their first child. They

Chad, Age 6 Months

named the baby Chad. The tiny infant thrilled the young couple.

Six months went by. Something seemed wrong. Chad wasn't crawling or rolling over. He kept dropping his rattle. He seemed cranky all the time. Worst of all, Chad began having seizures. Ron and Carly were frightened.

Muscular dystrophy is another condition that affects the muscles. It is different from cerebral palsy in two ways. First, muscular dystrophy is progressive. That means the condition keeps getting worse. Second, it is inherited.

Ron and Carly's baby showed symptoms, or evidence, of cerebral palsy. Some children with cerebral palsy have no obvious symptoms until they are toddlers or older. Other children, like Chad, show serious symptoms soon after birth.

The main symptoms of cerebral palsy involve muscles in three ways. One symptom is weak muscles. Another symptom is a lack of muscle tone in some muscles. The third symptom is a tightness of other muscles. Children need strong muscles to develop motor skills.

There are two kinds of motor skills. Gross motor skills use large muscle groups. These skills include balancing, reaching, sitting, crawling, and walking. Fine motor skills use small muscles in the fingers and hands. Such skills include drawing, writing, and grasping things.

Most children learn to perform various motor skills by a certain age. Children with cerebral palsy may be slow to develop motor skills. They may not develop them at all.

Other Signs of Cerebral Palsy

There are other important signs of cerebral palsy. An infant with cerebral palsy may:

Have difficulty sucking or swallowing

Use one side of the body more than the other

Have spasticity of some muscles

Lack energy

Have seizures

Be difficult to wake

Have problems with seeing and hearing

Be unusually tense and irritable

As a child with cerebral palsy grows, other symptoms might include:

Drooling

Difficulty with speech

Difficulty with bowel and bladder control

Hand tremors, or shakes

Inability to name objects by touch

Steps in Diagnosis

Doctors go through several steps in diagnosing cerebral palsy. Getting the child's medical history is the first step. Doctors ask about any problems during the mother's pregnancy or during the delivery. They also ask about any serious illnesses or conditions in the child's family. They compare the child's development with normal child development.

Here are important steps in a young child's physical development.

Gross Motor Skills

1 month	lifts head
3 months	can lie on chest
6 months	rolls and sits well without support
12 months	walks alone
18 months	walks up steps
24 months	alternates feet on stairs; kicks a ball

Fine Motor Skills

1 month	makes fist; stares at objects
3 months	grasps rattle placed in hand
6 months	reaches and grasps
12 months	grasps small objects
18 months	stacks three blocks; uses spoon
24 months	stacks six blocks; turns book pages

The second step is a physical exam. Doctors watch closely to see how the child uses his or her muscles. They check to see if muscle tone is tense, floppy, or spastic. They also look for abnormal movements such as jerkiness.

The third step is to conduct various tests. Laboratory tests such as blood work may rule out other causes of the child's motor problems. Brain pictures and other medical tests may show abnormalities in the brain. Scars on the brain indicate that the child is likely to have motor difficulties. Doctors also may order tests to determine the child's mental ability or level of speech.

Difficulties in Diagnosis

Diagnosing cerebral palsy can be difficult. There is no single test for the condition. Brain tumors, bone deformities, allergies, and other problems have similar symptoms. Sometimes the child has another major disability. For example, the child may be blind. Doctors may focus on dealing with the blindness.

Cerebral palsy also can cause doctors to misdiagnose a person's problem. For example, cerebral palsy can affect the muscles needed for speech. A child with cerebral palsy might have normal intelligence but be unable to talk. The child might be labeled mentally retarded.

Several skilled doctors may be needed to diagnose cerebral palsy in a child. These doctors may include:

A pediatrician—a doctor who specializes in the care of children

A developmental pediatrician—a doctor who specializes in child development

A pediatric neurologist—a doctor who specializes in disorders of the brain and nervous system in children

Time Line for Diagnosis

Cerebral palsy is rarely diagnosed at birth. All newborns lack muscle control. Their movements are reflex actions. This means that they happen on their own. Doctors generally wait until the child is between 15 and 24 months to make a diagnosis. By then, the child's motor problems are more apparent. Doctors can then make a more positive diagnosis of cerebral palsy.

New diagnostic techniques are pushing downward the age at which diagnosis is made. In some cases, a correct diagnosis now can be made before a child is one.

Chad, Age 9 Months

Ron and Carly took Chad to their pediatrician. She urged them to take the baby to a special center for developmental disorders. Chad was nine months old when his cerebral palsy was diagnosed.

The diagnosis shocked and scared Ron and Carly. They worried about their baby's future. Doctors put the couple in touch with an early-intervention program near their home. They said the sooner Chad started treatment, the better.

Chad began receiving occupational and physical therapy. Ron and Carly learned to do the exercises at home. They held up bright flash cards for him to grab. They moved his legs back and forth. They played games to improve his balance. When Chad grew older, he rode a special tricycle. The pedals moved his legs up and down.

Chad now goes to a preschool for children with special needs. Next year, he will start first grade in a regular school. Ron and Carly believe that Chad's progress is due to the early treatment. "Without it," Carly says, "he wouldn't be able to do half the things he can do now. He'd be sitting in a wheelchair."

Chad, Age 5

Cerebral Palsy

Ruth Sienkiewicz-Mercer is a person who was misdiagnosed. Cerebral palsy left her unable to speak. At age five, she was diagnosed as severely mentally retarded. Ruth spent her childhood in state hospitals for the retarded. One day, an aide noticed that Ruth laughed at a humorous story. Hospital officials began to suspect that Ruth was not retarded after all. You can read about her life in the book *I Raise My Eyes to Say Yes.*

Points to Consider

Have you or has a family member ever been diagnosed with a serious condition? How did you react?

When did you learn to roll over, crawl, walk, and talk? Ask your parents how they felt at each motor milestone. How might they have felt if you weren't reaching the milestones?

Why might the parents of a child with cerebral palsy feel guilty?

Chapter Overview

Cerebral palsy cannot be cured. The disabilities caused by cerebral palsy, however, can be managed. Things can be done to help people with cerebral palsy function better physically.

Physical therapists try to improve a person's overall movement. Occupational therapists work on motor skills needed for daily living activities. Speech therapists focus on language, speech, hearing, and swallowing.

Medications can help to reduce spasticity. Surgery also can help to relax muscles and correct deformities.

Many skilled professionals help people with cerebral palsy. Family and friends provide important support, too.

Chapter 4

Managing Cerebral Palsy

There is no cure for cerebral palsy, but some treatments can help to improve movement. People with cerebral palsy also can learn ways to adapt to their physical limitations.

Physical Therapy

Physical therapy for people with cerebral palsy works mainly on gross motor skills. Physical therapists train people in sitting, balancing, walking, and climbing stairs. They try to improve the person's muscle tone, posture, and balance. They also teach people with cerebral palsy to use braces, crutches, wheelchairs, and other aids.

Latisha has these tips to make dressing easier for wheelchair users:

- Dress in front of a mirror. It's easier to find the sleeves and match buttons and buttonholes.
- Button garments from the bottom up. You're less likely to miss a button.
- Dress the disabled arm or leg first. Undress the good limb first.
- Make openings larger. Replace short zippers with long zippers.

How often and how intensely people receive physical therapy depend on the individual. Young children benefit the most from ongoing therapy. Their brain still has the ability to finish the normal period of development. Teens and adults might take therapy on an as-needed basis. They might follow an exercise routine designed by a physical therapist.

Robin, Age 15

Robin has severe spastic diplegia. She is not able to walk. When Robin was younger, her parents paid for private physical therapy. Now Robin gets her therapy at public school. She takes an adaptive physical education class. Her therapy also is built into her activities all day. All of her teachers know things they can do to loosen, strengthen, and stretch her muscles.

Much of Robin's therapy is geared toward self-care. For example, she practices standing and holding onto a bar. This helps when she goes to the bathroom. She positions her wheelchair next to the toilet. Then she grabs the bar next to the toilet and pulls herself up. She hangs on to the bar to undo her clothes. Robin usually can manage her toileting needs without an aide.

There are many different approaches to physical therapy. Experienced therapists try several approaches. They follow the one that seems to work best for the individual child.

Occupational Therapy

Occupational therapy focuses on the muscle control and coordination needed for daily routines. Many of these tasks require fine motor skills and eye-hand coordination. This means the occupational therapists might work with people on eating, bathing, and dressing. They might work with older children on writing and using a computer. Teens and adults learn skills related to keeping house and holding a job.

Occupational therapists teach people with cerebral palsy techniques to make everyday life easier. For example, there are special tricks for getting dressed while sitting in a wheelchair. Occupational therapists also explain how to use daily living aids. Many devices are available to help with bathing, dressing, cooking, and eating.

Did You Know?

The tongue is a muscle. You need your tongue for speaking and eating.

Speech Therapy

Some people with cerebral palsy lack control of the muscles used in speech. They may have problems hearing correct speech sounds. As a result, they have difficulty speaking clearly. Speech therapists teach these people how to breathe and use the vocal cords to make sounds.

Some people with cerebral palsy are not able to speak at all. In these cases, speech therapists teach other ways of communicating. They may teach the person to use hand signals or eye movements. They may teach the person to use a special device. The device might be something simple, such as a symbol board or a picture board. The device might be something more complex, such as an electronic voice synthesizer. A synthesizer is an instrument that can imitate a variety of sounds.

Speech therapists also are trained to help people with swallowing problems. These therapists can help children with cerebral palsy learn how to eat.

Drug Therapy

Medications also are used to treat cerebral palsy. Some people take pills to relax their muscles. The effects generally last for just a few hours. The medication may cause drowsiness, confusion, and other side effects. Muscle relaxants also can be given by injection.

People with cerebral palsy may take medications for related conditions. They might take antiseizure medication to control seizures. Other medication helps control emotional and behavioral problems.

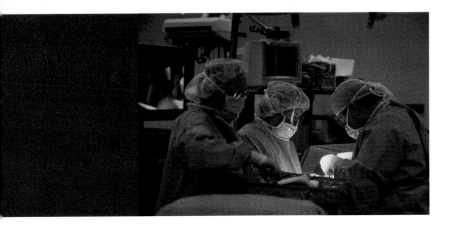

Surgery

Kyle used to feel like an old man. Cerebral palsy made the muscles in his back and legs very tight. He was too stooped over and pigeon-toed to play baseball. Worst of all, he could not take driver-education lessons.

Kyle, Age 17

Kyle went to a special hospital. The doctors there specialize in surgery that relaxes muscles and soft tissue. Kyle had three operations. Today he walks more normally. People no longer stare at him. Best of all, he got his driver's license.

In some cases, surgery can help people with cerebral palsy. Kyle had a type of surgery called rhizotomy. Surgeons cut some of the nerves along the spinal cord. This helps to reduce spasticity. Another type of surgery involves bones and joints. It is called orthopedic surgery. Surgeons lengthen muscles to improve mobility, or one's ability to move. Surgeons also correct bone and joint deformities. Many weeks of physical therapy follow surgery.

Cerebral Palsy

A special pump is now available to help people with severe spasticity. The pump is implanted beneath the skin of the abdomen. It delivers a muscle-relaxing drug directly into the spine. This method of delivery allows for much lower doses of medication. Lower doses reduce troublesome side effects. The pump is programmed to release medication at a rate suited for the individual.

The Management Team

Children and teens need many people to help manage their cerebral palsy. The team includes doctors, nurses, therapists, teachers, and social workers. Family members are an important part of the team, too. They can provide love and encouragement. They can help with therapy and medications at home, go along on doctors' appointments, and provide financial support.

As the child becomes older, he or she can become an active part of the management team as well. Teens with cerebral palsy should be involved in decisions about their health care.

Points to Consider

Do you know anyone who has had physical therapy? Why did that person need it? What did the therapy involve?

Imagine that you have difficulty controlling your muscles. What activities of daily living might be hard to do?

How could you be part of the management team for a friend with cerebral palsy?

Chapter Overview

Most people with disabilities want to be independent. They want to be able to support themselves and live on their own.

Assistive technology helps many people with cerebral palsy to function independently. These devices assist with tasks of daily living. They also help people with cerebral palsy to communicate and to have jobs.

Barrier-free buildings help people in wheelchairs to move about without assistance.

Special education programs assist people with cerebral palsy to get the best education possible.

Job training and independent living programs help to prepare people with cerebral palsy to live on their own.

Chapter 5

Becoming Independent

Many people with cerebral palsy want to be like everyone else. They want to be able to move about freely. They want to be able to take care of themselves. In the past, people with cerebral palsy had a hard time being independent. Special programs and equipment now enable them to be more independent. In addition, the public's attitude toward people with disabilities is changing. The focus has shifted from taking care of the disabled to helping them become self-sufficient.

People with limited or no speech now can use a telephone. Special software can turn a computer into a phone. Users enter words on a keyboard or other input device. The system converts text to speech and transmits it to other users.

Assistive Technology

Many special devices are available to aid people with cerebral palsy at home, work, school, and play. These pieces of equipment are known as assistive technology.

"Low-tech" assistive technology consists of simple devices. Many of these devices help with dressing, cooking, and eating. For example, people who have limited use of their hands might use elastic shoelaces. These laces permit shoes to be slipped on and off without tying or untying. Low-tech assistive technology includes devices that people with cerebral palsy invent for themselves.

"High-tech" assistive devices are more complicated. One example is a computer that allows people with limited or no speech to communicate. Also, vans with wheelchair lifts or cars with special controls can provide transportation for people with cerebral palsy. High-tech assistive devices are usually expensive. People need to be trained on how to use them for these devices to be most useful.

Barrier-Free Buildings

Barrier-free buildings allow people with disabilities to move about easily and safely. Laws now require that public buildings be accessible to people in wheelchairs. This means installing ramps and elevators. It also means having doors wide enough for a wheelchair to pass through. Doors should be easy to open or should open automatically. Public restrooms must have stalls and sinks that people in wheelchairs can use.

Special Education

Aaron has cerebral palsy. He also has a minor learning disability. He takes all **Aaron, Age 14** regular classes but goes to a special resource room for help with assignments. Aaron has some difficulty writing. His teachers give him extra time to take tests.

Most schools in the United States and Canada have special education programs. These programs are designed to meet the needs of children and teens with disabilities. As with any educational program, the long-term goal is to help students become self-sufficient.

Schools now mainstream special-needs students as much as possible. Mainstreaming means moving students with disabilities into regular classrooms. It also means including them in regular school activities such as eating in the lunchroom or riding the school bus.

Mainstreaming has several advantages for children and teens with disabilities. One advantage is the opportunity to develop social skills. Teens with cerebral palsy learn how to get along with others. They have a chance to make friends and have fun. Being able to interact with others is important for independent living.

Rob has severe cerebral palsy. He must use a **Rob, Age 17** wheelchair. He also has mental retardation.
Rob spends nearly all day in the special education room. He goes to a regular health class and to choir. Sharon, Rob's special education aide, accompanies him to these classes.

Rob rides in a regular school bus. The bus is equipped with a wheelchair lift. Rob enjoys being with the other kids. He loves to tell jokes and get in on the latest gossip. The kids on the bus sometimes get rowdy. Rob thinks this is fun, too. He feels like he's part of the action.

Cerebral Palsy

An electronic, push-button world makes life easier for people with cerebral palsy. Here are just a few examples. Can you think of others?
- TV remote control
- Automatic garage door opener
- Automatic can opener
- Cordless phone

Residential Programs

After high school, young adults with cerebral palsy might participate in a residential program. Several types of residential programs may be available in a community. In one type, the young adults take classes in grocery shopping, cooking, paying bills, and other independent living skills. Then a social worker or other trained professional helps them find an apartment.

In another type of residential program, the young adults live in a group home. A small group home might have four to six residents with disabilities. Trained staff also live in the house. They assist the residents with meal preparation and other daily living tasks.

Residential programs help young adults with cerebral palsy move from their parents' home to the outside world. It is sometimes difficult to learn to be independent while living at home. Parents may do too many things for their children. Children may not feel motivated to do more things for themselves. Residential programs encourage as much independence as possible.

Vocational Training

There is one very important way to be independent—having a job and earning a paycheck. Computer technology has created many job opportunities for people with cerebral palsy. These jobs generally involve handling information. They require less muscle strength than many other jobs.

Education and training are necessary for well-paying jobs. Many people with cerebral palsy enroll in regular two- and four-year college programs. Most communities also offer special job training programs for people with disabilities. These programs may take place at vocational schools and technical colleges. High schools, too, prepare students for the world of work.

Dionica participated in a work program **Dionica, Age 17** during the first quarter of her junior year in high school. Every noon, a van took her and several other students to a work site. At the work site, they did jobs for local businesses. For example, they rolled silverware in napkins for a hotel and assembled telephone receivers for a phone company. Dionica's supervisor evaluated her job skills. Dionica learned the importance of doing good work. Best of all, she got paid for her work.

Service dogs also help people with cerebral palsy to be independent. These specially trained dogs retrieve dropped objects. They also take items from shelves and open doors. They can even pay cashiers with specially designed billfolds.

Support Services

United Cerebral Palsy Associations and other organizations help people with cerebral palsy live independently. They help people find jobs and places to live. They help people find assistive technology. These organizations work for laws to improve the life of people with cerebral palsy. They also educate the public about cerebral palsy.

Points to Consider

Is your school building accessible to students and teachers with physical disabilities? Give examples of pluses and minuses.

What do you know about the special education program in your school? Do you have friends who are in special education? Do you think special education students should be mainstreamed? Why or why not?

How can a person's attitude be a block to his or her independence?

Chapter Overview

Teens with cerebral palsy experience the normal problems of growing up. Cerebral palsy can add to these problems.

Teens with cerebral palsy may have to deal with rude comments and teasing. Other people may avoid them. Teens with cerebral palsy may have difficulty making friends and fitting in.

Cerebral palsy can create problems for parents, brothers, and sisters.

Teens with cerebral palsy can learn to cope with problems. They can meet difficulties head on. Families, friends, and many skilled professionals are available to help.

Chapter 6

Living With Cerebral Palsy

The teenage years can be difficult for any teenager. They may be especially difficult for teens with cerebral palsy.

Getting Teased

Some people say cruel things about people with disabilities. They might call a person with cerebral palsy names. They might stare at a person with cerebral palsy in public. All this can hurt a great deal.

Many schools have programs to help students learn about disabilities. One school sponsors a class called "Insights on Disabilities." Students with disabilities meet with nondisabled students to explain what it is like to have a disability.

Teens with cerebral palsy have different ways of handling these situations. One teen sticks up for herself and stares right back. Another ignores the teasing of others. He hopes they will get tired and quit. Chelsea found another way.

Chelsea, Age 14

One day a couple of kids were making fun of Chelsea. They called her stupid and said she should be in kindergarten. Chelsea talked to the school counselor. The counselor spoke to the students who had been bothering Chelsea. They apologized to her. Chelsea explained to them about cerebral palsy. The students stopped teasing her.

Telling Others

Teens with cerebral palsy may wonder what to tell others about their condition.

Scott, Age 17

Scott speaks very slowly because of his cerebral palsy. He used to dread meeting people for the first time. They always looked surprised and embarrassed when they heard him talk. Now Scott explains about his voice right away. This seems to help everyone relax.

Some people feel uncomfortable around people with disabilities. They do not know how to act or what to say. This is because they do not understand disabilities. Teens with cerebral palsy can educate others about their condition. The more people know about cerebral palsy, the better.

Fitting In

Teens with cerebral palsy want to be like other teens. This is not always possible. Having a disability makes them different. Teens with cerebral palsy need to realize that it is all right to be different. They can develop self-esteem by focusing on their abilities, not their disabilities. People with positive self-esteem are happy to be themselves.

Making Friends

Teens with cerebral palsy may have difficulty making friends. Speech and hearing problems can get in the way of friendships. Some teens do not want to be friends with someone who is different. Teens with cerebral palsy should try to be as active as possible. They might play sports or join clubs. They are bound to meet people who accept others just the way they are.

Sexuality

Teens with cerebral palsy can have crushes or fall in love just like anyone else. Some people may think that people with cerebral palsy cannot or do not have sexual relationships. These people are wrong. People with cerebral palsy may want to date, marry, or become parents. They can do these things. Teens with cerebral palsy may or may not decide to have a sexual relationship. They are equally at risk for pregnancy or sexually transmitted diseases as other teens are. These are diseases passed through sexual contact.

Dealing With Feelings

Most teenagers feel angry and depressed from time to time. Teens with cerebral palsy may experience these feelings more often. They may feel frustrated over their inability to do some things. They may feel they are a burden to others. They may feel inferior. Being teased or treated like a baby adds to feelings of anger and depression. Teens with cerebral palsy must learn to deal with negative feelings.

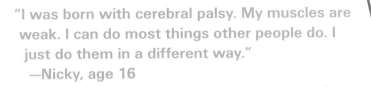
"Sometimes I wish I didn't have a disability. But I have to accept it. If I didn't have cerebral palsy, I wouldn't be me. I am happy with who I am."
—Kingston, age 15

"I was born with cerebral palsy. My muscles are weak. I can do most things other people do. I just do them in a different way."
—Nicky, age 16

Cerebral Palsy and the Family

Living with cerebral palsy can be difficult for a teen's family, too. Parents may feel guilty. They may believe they caused the teen's cerebral palsy. Parents may worry about their son or daughter's future. They may be afraid to let the teen go places and do things. This causes conflict when the teen wants to be more independent. Managing the problems related to cerebral palsy also takes a lot of hard work. Parents may become exhausted caring for a child or teen with cerebral palsy.

Brothers and sisters may have a hard time dealing with cerebral palsy as well. Parents tend to give more time and attention to children with special needs. Brothers and sisters may resent this. They may feel a duty to care for their sibling. They may overprotect him or her. They may feel guilty that they don't have cerebral palsy.

Fortunately, resources are available to help families cope with cerebral palsy. These include counseling and support groups for parents and siblings. Resources also include books and videos. All family members can grow as a result of living with a child with cerebral palsy.

Coping With Cerebral Palsy

Every person has some sort of problem. It is important to accept the problem, learn to cope, and get on with life. If you are a teen with cerebral palsy, here are some ways to cope:

Take an active part in managing your condition.
Work with your doctors, teachers, therapists, and other members of your management team. Learn all you can about cerebral palsy.

Act as your own agent in school.
Let your teachers know your needs. Let them know if your condition changes.

Discuss feelings of anger and sadness with a professional counselor.
Do not let these feelings get the best of you.

Join a support group for teens with disabilities.
If there is no group in your area, ask a teacher or counselor to help you start one. A support group can help you deal with problems and feelings. You can learn how others handle difficult situations. Support groups also offer recreation.

Adaptive driver education is available in some parts of the country. Check with your local chapter of United Cerebral Palsy Associations.

Did You Know?

Develop close friendships with a few people.
This is better than trying to be friends with everyone. Close friends understand and care about you. They know how to help.

Take training in independent living.
Learn to do all you can by yourself. Learn how to direct untrained individuals who want to help you. Find or make your own assistive devices.

Understand your rights as a person with cerebral palsy.
Join an organization that fights for the rights of people with disabilities. Stand up for what you need.

Do not let cerebral palsy be the focus of your life.
Develop hobbies and interests. Get involved in your community. Volunteer to help others.

Points to Consider

Has anyone ever made fun of you? How did you handle the teasing?

How does your school attempt to educate students about disabilities?

How could you help a teen with cerebral palsy strengthen his or her self-esteem?

Chapter Overview

Research on cerebral palsy continues in the areas of prevention, detection, treatment, and services.

Some of the causes of cerebral palsy can be reduced or eliminated. Expectant mothers can take good care of themselves. Parents and caregivers can protect infants and toddlers from accidents and injury.

Advances in the hospital delivery and care of newborns help prevent brain injury.

Much can be done to help people with cerebral palsy live satisfying lives. Public acceptance is very important.

Chapter 7

Looking Ahead

People once thought nothing could be done about cerebral palsy. This idea has changed. Now people know it is possible to take steps to help prevent cerebral palsy. It also is possible to make life better for those already affected. Many efforts are under way to make the future brighter for people with cerebral palsy.

Research

Much research is being done on cerebral palsy. One area of research focuses on the causes and prevention of cerebral palsy. Researchers attempt to answer many questions such as:

Is it possible to protect the developing brain of a fetus, or unborn baby? Is there a way to protect the newborn brain?

What causes lack of oxygen to the developing fetal brain?

What role does infection play in causing cerebral palsy?

Can cerebral palsy be diagnosed before birth? Can it be diagnosed better shortly after birth?

Why are low birth-weight, multiple-birth, and premature infants at risk for cerebral palsy?

Magnesium sulfate may prevent cerebral palsy in premature infants. Researchers are studying women who received this drug when they were in premature labor. The studies show fewer cases of cerebral palsy among the tiny infants born to these women. More research is necessary, however.

Into the
Future

Another area of research focuses on improving the quality of life for people with cerebral palsy. Researchers attempt to answer such questions as:

Which treatments are most effective for specific types of cerebral palsy?

How can medications and surgery be improved to relieve the symptoms of cerebral palsy?

How can educational and vocational programs be improved to help people with cerebral palsy?

How does aging affect people with cerebral palsy?

In the United States, four organizations lead research on cerebral palsy. One is the United Cerebral Palsy Research and Educational Foundation, a private organization. The other three are government organizations: the National Institutes of Health; the Centers for Disease Control and Prevention; and the National Institute for Disability and Rehabilitation Research.

Into the Future

Undiagnosed infections in a pregnant woman can cause cerebral palsy. New research is focused on learning which infections cause it and how to diagnose and treat those infections.

Prevention

Melanie began using drugs and alcohol at age 12. She became addicted to crack cocaine when she was 15. Melanie did not know she was pregnant until she went into premature labor. Her baby boy weighed less than 2 pounds. His condition was critical.

Melanie, Age 15

Doctors and nurses cared for him in a special intensive care unit for newborns. They saved the tiny infant's life. It was too late, however, to stop the brain damage. Melanie's baby had multiple birth defects, including cerebral palsy.

A healthy mother and good prenatal care can reduce the chances of premature delivery and low birth-weight babies. These are risk factors for cerebral palsy. Long before her childbearing years, a young woman should establish good eating and exercise habits. Before pregnancy, she should be immunized against German measles and other infections. To be immunized means she will become resistant to these infections.

Cerebral Palsy

During pregnancy, expectant mothers should eat nutritious, well-balanced meals, get plenty of rest, and avoid alcohol, tobacco products and other drugs. Regular visits to the doctor are extremely important. The doctor can monitor the development of the fetus and try to correct any problems.

Improvements in hospital labor and delivery rooms also help to prevent cerebral palsy. Sensitive instruments alert doctors and nurses to problems. New procedures make delivery safer and assure an adequate supply of oxygen to the infant. Incubators keep premature babies alive and healthy. Some hospitals have built high-tech units for the care of high-risk newborns.

Things also can be done to prevent cerebral palsy from occurring later in infancy. Parents and other caregivers can make sure the child's environment is safe. This includes keeping household cleaning products and other poisons out of the child's reach. It also includes using infant seats, seat belts, and helmets. These safety devices reduce the chances of head injury in a car or bicycle accident. Children also should be immunized against childhood diseases.

Education

Therapies, medications, and surgery help people with cerebral palsy improve muscle control. Educational and vocational training programs prepare them for jobs. Assistive technology and barrier-free buildings help them to be independent. Something else is needed for people with cerebral palsy to be successful—the acceptance of the public. The public needs to accept people with disabilities as employees and as equal participants in the community.

Do you wonder how to treat a person with a disability? The answer? Like a person! Be willing to listen, work and play, and even argue with that person!

Ernie, Age 16

Ernie's high school sponsors a "buddy" program. The program pairs a student with a disability and a nondisabled student. Students with disabilities have an opportunity to develop social skills. Nondisabled students learn what it is like to have a disability.

Ernie was paired with Ted, a classmate with cerebral palsy. The two boys met in a study room in the library. At first Ernie and Ted's meetings were awkward. Ernie got impatient when Ted talked. After a few times, Ernie relaxed and waited patiently for Ted to finish speaking. Ernie asked Ted questions if he didn't understand.

Ernie discovered that Ted had an amazing knowledge about sports. Ernie and Ted had each found a new friend.

Points to Consider

How can you help promote awareness of cerebral palsy?

How can you help people who are already affected by cerebral palsy?

What classes are offered in your community to help people learn more about cerebral palsy? Check with local cerebral palsy organizations.

Glossary

cerebral (suh-REE-bruhl or SER-uh-bruhl)—referring to the brain

chronic (KRON-ik)—continuing for a long time; a person with a chronic disease or illness may have it throughout life.

contagious (kuhn-TAY-juhss)—capable of being spread from person to person

contract (kuhn-TRAKT)—to become shorter; muscles contract to produce motion.

fetal (FEE-tuhl)—relating to a fetus

fetus (FEE-tuhss)—a developing human from three months after conception, or the date the mother becomes pregnant, to birth

immunize (IM-yuh-nize)—to make someone able to resist a disease or infection

motor (MOH-tur)—relating to movement

palsy (PAWL-zee)—referring to muscle weakness

premature (PREE-muh-choor)—happening before the intended time

prenatal (pree-NAY-tuhl)—occurring before birth

seizure (see-zhur)—sudden, abnormal activity in the brain

spasm (SPAZM)—a sudden tightening of a muscle that cannot be controlled

spastic (SPASS-tik)—the most common type of cerebral palsy; muscles become tight and stiff.

tone (TOHN)—the tension in a muscle at rest

For More Information

Aaseng, Nathan. *Cerebral Palsy.* New York: Franklin Watts, 1991.

Huegel, Kelly. *Young People and Chronic Illness.* Minneapolis: Free Spirit, 1998.

Kent, Deborah. *The Disability Rights Movement.* Danbury, CT: Children's Press, 1996.

LeVert, Suzanne. *Teens Face to Face With Chronic Illness.* New York: Julian Messner, 1993.

Useful Addresses and Internet Sites

National Information Center for Children and
Youth with Disabilities
PO Box 1492
Washington, DC 20013-1492
1-800-695-0285

Ontario Federation for Cerebral Palsy
1630 Lawrence Avenue West, Suite 104
Toronto, ON M6L 1C5
CANADA

United Cerebral Palsy Associations
UCP Research and Educational Foundation
1660 L Street Northwest, Suite 700
Washington, DC 20036-5602
1-800-872-5827

United States Cerebral Palsy Athletic
Association
25 West Independence Way
Kingston, RI 02881

March of Dimes Birth Defects Foundation
http://www.modimes.org
Provides information on preventing birth
defects

National Information Center for Children and
Youth with Disabilities
http://www.nichcy.org
Provides information on disabilities for
families, educators, and professionals

Ontario Federation for Cerebral Palsy
http:// www.ofcp,on.ca
Provides information on the changing needs of
people with cerebral palsy

United Cerebral Palsy Associations
http://www.ucpa.org
Provides information on programs and services
for people with cerebral palsy and on medical
research as well

Index

Index continued